S0-ABD-654

N/A

0 C10

Exploring
CANYONS

Melody S. Mis

PowerKiDS press™

New York

To Barbara Jean Heavener Moon

Published in 2009 by The Rosen Publishing Group, Inc.
29 East 21st Street, New York, NY 10010

First Edition

Editor: Nicole Pristash
Book Design: Julio Gil
Photo Researcher: Jessica Gerweck

Photo Credits: Cover, pp. 5, 7, 9, 11, 15, 17, 19, 21 Shutterstock.com; p. 13 © Antoni Georges/Age Fotostock.

Library of Congress Cataloging-in-Publication Data

Mis, Melody S.
  Exploring canyons / Melody S. Mis. — 1st ed.
      p. cm. — (Geography zone. Landforms)
  Includes index.
  ISBN 978-1-4358-2716-5 (library binding) — ISBN 978-1-4358-3114-8 (pbk.)
ISBN 978-1-4358-3120-9 (6-pack)
  1. Canyons—Juvenile literature. 2. Grand Canyon (Ariz)—Juvenile literature. 3. Canyon plants—Juvenile literature. 4. Canyon animals—Juvenile literature. I. Title.
  GB562.M57 2009
  551.44'2—dc22

                                               2008029128

Manufactured in the United States of America

Contents

A canyon is a deep valley in between cliffs. Canyons have steep sides. They are found in rocky places and on the ocean floor. A canyon is often called a gorge.

Have you ever heard of the Grand Canyon, in Arizona? The Grand Canyon is the deepest canyon in the United States. It is around 1 mile (2 km) deep.

There are a lot of things to learn about canyons, such as the ways canyons are formed and what plants and animals live inside them. Let's take a closer look at canyons and **explore** some of these interesting landforms!

This is Geikie Gorge, in western Australia. Geikie Gorge is one of the best-known canyons in Australia, and it is a common place to visit.

Canyons are formed by **erosion**. Water erosion is the most common way a canyon is formed. When a lot of rain falls and when snow melts, the water forms streams and rivers. These streams and rivers then flow downhill over rock toward an ocean or a lake.

As the water moves, it carries sand and soil with it. The sand and soil act like **sandpaper** by rubbing against the rock over and over again. This rubbing causes the rock to erode, and deep cuts are made. Over a long period of time, these deep cuts can become canyons.

Marble Canyon was formed by the Colorado River. The Colorado River flows 1,450 miles (2,333.5 km), from Colorado to the Gulf of California.

Weathering is another way canyons are formed. Weathering is the erosion of rock by wind, ice, and other weather.

Wind causes weathering as it blows sand against rock. The blowing sand wears the rock away over time. Water causes weathering when it becomes ice inside holes in rock. The ice can cause the rock to break **apart**. Hot and cold weather cause weathering, too. The Sun heats rock during the day. At night, the rock gets cold. This change can also cause the rock to break apart.

Weathering and water erosion happen every day. These actions are what shape different types of canyons.

Here you can see how weathering has caused pieces of rock to break off over time in this canyon.

A slot canyon is a canyon that is deep but very narrow at the top. From the air, a slot canyon looks like a skinny gap in the earth. The walls inside slot canyons are often red or purple.

Most slot canyons are **carved** out of sandstone. Sandstone is rock made from hardened sand. First, gaps in the sandstone fill with water, and the water erodes the sandstone. The gaps then get deeper as more water flows through, forming a slot canyon.

Slot canyons are common in the western United States. The state of Utah has more than 1,000 slot canyons.

This is Upper Antelope Canyon, in Arizona. The smooth and colorful walls of the canyon rise around 120 feet (37 m) above the floor.

Canyons can be found on the ocean floor, too. An underwater canyon often begins as a piece of land. However, water from a river can slowly erode the land and form a canyon. Then, when the sea rises, the sea covers the canyon and the land around it. As more ocean water moves through the canyon, it erodes the canyon even more.

One of the deepest underwater canyons is called the Great Bahama Canyon. It is in the Atlantic Ocean near the Bahamas. The Great Bahama Canyon is 14,060 feet (4,285 m) deep and 140 miles (225 km) long.

An underwater canyon, like this one, is a common place for divers to explore. Underwater canyons often have a lot of plants and fish in them.

Canyons are often found in places that are hot and dry, such as deserts. Deserts do not receive much rain, so only certain types of plants grow there.

Cacti often grow in desert canyons. A cactus is a plant that does not need much water to grow. The prickly pear is an example of a cactus plant. The prickly pear stores water inside it, so it can grow in such hot weather.

Other plants grow in canyons that get more rain. Wildflowers, pine trees, and fir trees are just some of the plants that grow in wetter canyons.

This picture shows prickly pear cacti growing in Canyonlands National Park, in Utah. Prickly pears are green with red, purple, or yellow flowers.

Most desert canyons are hot during the day and cool at night. Different animals are **active** in a canyon during these two times of day. Deer, coyotes, and rabbits come out in the morning before it gets too hot. Squirrels, snakes, and eagles look for food later in the day. They like the hot, dry weather.

Rats, skunks, and mountain lions come out at night when it is cool. They do not like to look for food when it is hot. Bears visit canyons in the fall. They like to eat the fruit of the prickly pear cactus.

In the morning, deer feed on leaves, grasses, and branches around the canyon. During the hot afternoon, deer find shade to keep cool.

The best-known canyon in America is the Grand Canyon, in northwestern Arizona. It is 277 miles (446 km) long, making it one of the largest canyons in the world. The Grand Canyon has around 40 **layers** of rock. The main types of rock in those layers are sandstone, limestone, and shale. Limestone is made of small sea animals that have died. Shale is hardened mud.

The rock in the Grand Canyon began forming over one **billion** years ago. The Colorado River then slowly carved the canyon out of the rock. In fact, the river is still carving the canyon today!

A study shows that the Colorado River may have begun carving the Grand Canyon around 17 million years ago.

From the top of the Grand Canyon, it may look empty. However, there is a lot of life inside its walls. Forests of pine trees grow at the top of the canyon. Deer, mountain lions, and wild turkeys live there. Cactus plants and pink rattlesnakes live at the bottom. Pink rattlesnakes do not live anywhere else on Earth!

Native Americans have lived in the Grand Canyon for 4,000 years. **Ancient** Native Americans grew vegetables there, and they made baskets from the yucca plant. Yuccas are tall plants with white flowers. Today, Native Americans, called the Havasu 'Baaja, live in the canyon.

Horned lizards do not mind the hot weather inside the Grand Canyon. These lizards are often active during the hottest part of the day.

People often visit canyons. Many of America's popular canyons are in national parks. These canyons are being kept safe for people to enjoy for years to come.

People like canyons because of the scenery. Some people enjoy **hiking** and rock climbing in canyons. Brave people even ride **mules** along narrow paths down into the Grand Canyon.

Canyons are some of Earth's oldest landforms. If you ever visit a canyon, look at the layers of rock, the plants, and the animals around you. Canyons are special, and they will be around for a long time for us to enjoy!

Glossary

active (AK-tiv) Busy or moving.

ancient (AYN-shent) Very old, from a long time ago.

apart (uh-PAHRT) Into parts or pieces.

billion (BIL-yun) One thousand millions.

carved (KAHRVD) Cut into a shape.

erosion (ih-ROH-zhun) The wearing away of land over time.

explore (ek-SPLOR) To go over carefully.

hiking (HYK-ing) Walking for a long time, generally in the mountains or the country.

layers (LAY-erz) Thicknesses of something.

mules (MYOOLZ) Animals that are part horse and part donkey.

sandpaper (SAND-pay-per) Paper covered with sand used to rub things to make them smooth.

Index

A

animals, 4, 16, 18, 22
Arizona, 4, 18

C

cliffs, 4

E

erosion, 6, 8

G

gorge, 4
Grand Canyon, 4, 18, 20, 22

L

layers, 18, 22

M

mules, 22

N

Native Americans, 20

P

places, 4, 14
plants, 4, 14, 20, 22

R

river(s), 6, 12, 18
rock, 6, 8, 10, 18, 22

S

sandstone, 10, 18
snow, 6

U

United States, 4, 10

V

valley, 4

Web Sites

Due to the changing nature of Internet links, PowerKids Press has developed an online list of Web sites related to the subject of this book. This site is updated regularly. Please use this link to access the list:
www.powerkidslinks.com/gzone/canyon/